Python for Teens: A Step-by-Step Guide

© 2023 by Dr. Leo Lexicon

iii

Python for Teens:
A Step-by-Step Guide

by

Dr. Leo Lexicon

Python for Teens:
A Step-by-Step Guide

Python is one of the most popular and versatile programming languages used today. Python for Teens provides a comprehensive yet accessible introduction to Python tailored for teenagers and beginners. This book will take you from writing your first Python script all the way to building real-world applications and tools.

The book begins with an overview of programming basics, installation, and a simple "Hello World" script to get started. It then covers core Python syntax like variables, data types, operators, loops, functions, and OOP concepts. Practical examples make these concepts easy to grasp. Advanced topics like list comprehensions, decorators, and exception handling prepare you for real Python development.

The book features hands-on coding projects including a calculator, text adventure game, web scraper, and data visualization tools. These projects help reinforce what you've learned in a practical manner. The final chapter discusses next steps like contributing to open source and potential Python career paths in fields like machine learning and web development.

Overall, Python for Teens provides the essential knowledge and skills teenagers need to learn Python programming. The step-by-step approach, ample examples, and hands-on projects make Python accessible and fun to learn. Readers will gain the confidence and ability to build real-world Python applications by the end. Both beginners and those with some prior coding experience can benefit from this book.

Dr. Leo Lexicon is an educator and author. He is the founder of Lexicon Labs, a publishing imprint that is focused on creating entertaining and educational books for active minds.

CONTENTS

Chapter 1: Introduction to Python

Python is one of the most versatile, user-friendly, and powerful programming languages used today. From software development to machine learning to data analysis, Python plays a role in countless applications and technologies. As a teenager interested in coding, Python is an excellent language to start your programming journey.

This book, Python for Teenagers: A Step-by-Step Guide to Learning Python, provides everything you need to go from writing your first Python program to building real-world apps and tools. By the end, you'll have the skills and confidence to take on Python projects for fun, school, or even as a career path down the road.

Who This Book Is For

Python for Teenagers is tailored for complete beginners who want to learn coding and Python. No prior programming experience is required. The book takes a step-by-step approach, starting with the fundamentals before gradually introducing more advanced concepts. Along the way, we use analogies, visual diagrams, and plain English explanations to make technical topics approachable.

As teenagers, you are at the perfect age to begin programming. Your mind is primed for logical thinking and problem solving - both core skills in computer science. Python is also well-suited for beginners given its straightforward syntax, abundance of libraries, and wide range of applications.

Whether you're looking for a fun hobby, want to boost your STEM skills, or hope to pursue coding in the future - Python is a great starting point. This book provides everything you need to turn coding into a passion and set you up for programming success.

What You Will Achieve

By the end of this book, you will gain:
- Strong foundational knowledge of core programming concepts like variables, data structures, functions, and object-oriented principles
- Proficiency in Python syntax, constructs, and best practices for writing clean code
- The ability to build practical Python programs from scratch to solve problems or automate tasks
- Hands-on experience creating real-world apps like calculators, games, web scrapers, and data visualizations
- Understanding of more advanced Python features like list comprehensions, lambda functions, and decorators
- Skills for troubleshooting bugs, reading error messages, and problem solving like an experienced coder
- Confidence in your programming abilities along with resources for further developing your Python skills

The book aims to take you from a complete beginner to having intermediate Python skills. While we don't cover every advanced topic, you'll have the core knowledge to expand your abilities. You'll also pick up essential programming concepts that apply to many languages.

Overview of Tools

To follow along and practice your Python coding skills, you will need:

- A computer running Windows, Mac OSX, or Linux
- Internet access for installing software and packages
- The latest version of Python installed on your computer
- A text editor for writing code like VS Code, Atom, Sublime Text, etc.
- Optional: a GitHub account for sharing and collaborating on code

We will cover how to setup these tools in Chapter 1. No specialized hardware or expensive software is required. All the tools we use are completely free.

Your computer likely comes pre-installed with an older version of Python. We recommend installing the latest Python version which will give you access to newer features and modules. Python also maintains excellent backwards compatibility so older Python tutorials and documentation will still apply to the newer versions.

For the text editor, you can use any programmer-focused editor you like. We suggest free and open source options like Visual Studio Code, Atom, Sublime Text, and Notepad++. These editors make writing and running Python code easy. Don't use basic text editors like Notepad (Windows) or TextEdit (Mac) which lack programming support.

Having a GitHub account is optional but highly recommended. GitHub hosts code online and lets you share your projects with others. It's used by millions of developers to collaborate on software. We'll cover GitHub basics in the book so you can put your own Python projects on GitHub!

Overview of the Chapters

Now let's briefly overview the key topics covered in the remaining chapters:

Chapter 2: Setting the Stage

This chapter gets you fully setup to start coding in Python. We'll cover:

- What exactly programming and coding are
- How programs provide instructions to computers
- Brief history of programming and how languages evolved
- Overview of popular programming languages and their uses
- What makes Python such a widely used and versatile language
- Installation guide for Python on Windows, Mac, and Linux
- Installation guide for a code editor like VS Code
- Writing your first Python program to print "Hello World!"

By the end, you'll have Python installed, an editor setup, and experience running a simple script.

Chapter 3: Python Syntax and Structure

In this chapter, we dig into the building blocks of Python code:
- Using variables to store data in memory
- Data types like strings, integers, booleans, lists, and dictionaries
- Arithmetic, comparison, and logical operators
- Rules for indentation, code structure, and style
- Adding comments to document your code
- Multi-line strings and documentation using docstrings

We'll also create simple programs to demonstrate these core concepts. You'll get exposure to real Python syntax hands-on.

Chapter 4: Conditional Statements and Loops

This chapter introduces control flow - making your programs respond intelligently based on different conditions:

- If, else if, and else statements to execute code selectively
- While loops to repeat code as long as a condition holds true
- For loops to iterate through sequences like lists and dictionaries
- Break, continue, pass, and other statements for additional loop control

We'll use these constructs to create programs that make decisions and repeat tasks efficiently. You'll start to see how even simple logic translates into powerful and complex programs.

Chapter 5: Functions and Modules

Functions and modules are key components of code organization and reuse:
- Defining reusable functions with parameters and return values
- Variables scope and namespaces
- Importing code modules like math, random, statistics, etc.
- Creating custom modules and packages
- Standard Python modules for common programming tasks

We'll write functions to abstract away repetitive code. You'll learn to tap into the vast ecosystem of Python modules for saving time and effort.

Chapter 6: Working with Data

This chapter explores built-in Python data structures and techniques for handling data:
- Lists and tuples for storing ordered data
- Sets and dictionaries for unordered data lookup
- Reading and writing files like CSVs, JSON, and text
- Built-in methods for data wrangling and cleansing
- Exception handling with try/except blocks

You'll gain hands-on experience working with real dataset files and formats. We'll also cover techniques like list comprehensions for managing data efficiently.

Chapter 7: Intermediate Python Concepts

We'll now take a step up to more advanced Python programming topics:
- List, dictionary, and set comprehensions
- Anonymous lambda functions

- Recursion with function calls
- Methods as objects using decorators
- Classes and object-oriented programming
- Catching and handling errors smoothly

These topics demonstrate the true power and versatility of Python. You'll level up your skills and be able to read and understand more complex Python code.

Chapter 8: Building Python Projects

In this chapter, we integrate all the concepts learned so far into building real Python applications and tools:
- Simple command line calculator
- Text-based adventure game
- Web scraper to extract data
- Data visualization with Matplotlib
- CRUD application with file database

You'll gain experience taking a program from conception through completion. These projects will reinforce your Python skills while allowing you to build an impressive coding portfolio.

Chapter 9: Moving Forward

In our final chapter, we discuss next steps on your Python journey:
- Expanding your skills through practice and coding challenges
- Contributing to open source Python projects on GitHub
- Exploring popular Python frameworks like Django and Flask
- Useful Python modules like NumPy, Pandas, TensorFlow, and more
- Options for Python certifications and careers

We'll leave you equipped with the knowledge, skills, and resources to continue growing as a Python programmer. The possibilities are endless!

In summary, this book provides a 360-degree education in Python. You'll go from beginner to intermediate level, building real code and apps along the way. The book aims not just to teach Python syntax, but also programming fundamentals that apply to any language. Upon finishing, you'll have the skills to expand your coding abilities on your own - and hopefully a newfound passion for programming!

Now, let's begin our Python journey

Chapter 2: Setting the Stage

Taking the First Steps

Welcome to the world of coding and Python! In this chapter, we'll cover the basics of programming and Python to get you set up and started on your journey.

We'll begin with an introduction to key programming concepts before looking at why Python is such a great first language to learn. We'll then walk through installing Python and a code editor on your computer. By the end of the chapter, you'll run your first real Python script and print "Hello World!" - the official initiation to coding!
Ready? Let's dive in!

Introduction to Programming Languages

So what exactly is programming? And how do computers understand code to do useful things?

Programming refers to the process of writing instructions for a computer to perform specific tasks. The instructions are written in special languages designed for software development. These languages are logically structured so that a computer can understand them.

Some common analogies for programming include:
- Following a recipe - Each instruction is a step needed to create the final product.
- Writing a manual - Explaining how to accomplish a task in discrete steps.
- Composing music - Programming languages have grammatical rules and syntax.

Programmers use language keywords, syntax, variables, data structures, and logical operators to write instructions that a computer can interpret and execute. For example, an instruction in Python might look like:

```
print("Hello World!")
```

This line uses the `print()` function and a string argument to output text to the user. The computer runs this line and displays the words "Hello World!" as we instructed.

[**Note**: For your convenience, and to enhance readability, the text in the black box, as well as other relevant snippets are shown in a slightly larger font size]

Without a programming language, we'd have to give computers instructions using purely numeric machine code. Programming languages allow us to write in a format that's readable while still being translatable to machine code.

Hundreds of programming languages exist today with new ones frequently being created. Some popular options include:

Python: General purpose language, easy for beginners to learn

JavaScript: Primary language for web development

C++: Used for high performance software like games

Java: Popular for business applications and Android development

SQL: Language for managing databases

R: Used for statistical analysis and data science

Swift: Apple's language for creating iOS apps

Each language has strengths and uses based on its syntax, ecosystem, and community. As a beginner, Python is excellent to start with due to its simplicity, versatility, and huge community. Later in your coding journey, you may learn other languages for specific use cases. But Python skills will take you very far on their own.

Now that we have a high-level sense of what programming is, let's look closer at why Python is a great first choice.

Why Choose Python?

Python has exploded in popularity in recent years. It consistently ranks as one of the top 3 most used languages along with Java and JavaScript. Python dates back to 1989 when developer Guido van Rossum created it as a general purpose scripting language. The name "Python" actually comes from the British comedy group Monty Python - not the snake! Since its creation, Python has grown into one of the most capable and versatile languages used today. Here are some key reasons why Python is a great first language to learn for beginners:

Simplicity and Readability

Python uses clear, natural language keywords and syntax. This makes Python very readable and intuitive compared to languages like Java that use strict, dense syntax. Python's syntax rules also result in less lines of code compared to other languages.

For example, here is how you print "Hello World!" in Java vs Python.

```
// Java
public class HelloWorld {
    public static void main(String[] args) {
        System.out.println("Hello World!");
    }
}
```

```
}
# Python
print("Hello World!")
```

As you can see, Python is far more concise and straightforward for simple tasks. This makes it easier to learn for coding beginners.

Huge Community and Ecosystem

Python has one of the largest developer communities worldwide. This means tons of open source Python libraries and tools are available for you as a new coder!

Popular resources like Stack Overflow have hundreds of thousands of Python-related questions and answers. Whatever issue you run into, chances are other people have solved it.

A large community also means more tutorials, documentation, and learning resources exist for Python. You'll have plenty of support on your Python journey.

Versatility for Multiple Use Cases

One of Python's greatest strengths is its versatility across many programming domains:

- Web development - Build websites and APIs with Django and Flask
- Data science - Data analysis and machine learning using NumPy, Pandas, SciPy
- Automation - Scripting and task automation with libraries like Selenium
- Software testing - Writing test suites in Python
- General purpose - Scripting, prototyping, and more

This versatility makes Python a great language to start with. The skills you learn can be applied across many types of programming you may want to get into.

Abundance of Libraries and Frameworks

Python has a vast collection of open source libraries and frameworks for different tasks, like:

- Data visualization (Matplotlib, Seaborn)
- GUI development (PyQt, Tkinter)
- Web scraping (Beautiful Soup, Scrapy)
- Image processing (OpenCV, Pillow)

As a beginner, you can utilize these tools to build powerful applications without needing to be an expert coder yet. Python's abundance of packages allows you to focus on problem solving vs low level details.

Growing Demand and Job Opportunities

Python is one of the most in-demand programming skills. Tech job listings for Python grew by 456% from 2010 to 2019 (Dice Insights). Knowing Python can open up opportunities in fields like:

- Web development
- Data science
- Machine learning
- Automation and testing
- Analytics
- Security

Given Python's versatility, it is a great language to have on your resume regardless of your specialty. Learning Python early on can set you up well for future tech careers if you choose to pursue them.

In summary, Python is beginner-friendly but also powerful and capable of professional applications. It's the perfect first language to start your programming journey with.

Now let's look at how to get set up with Python on your computer.

Installing Python

One of the first steps to using Python is having it installed on your computer.

Python comes pre-installed on many Linux and Mac systems. For Windows, you'll need to install it yourself. We recommend installing the latest Python 3 release for access to the newest features and modules.

Here are instructions for installing Python on different operating systems:

Windows

Download the latest Python 3 installer from python.org. Be sure to get the 64-bit version on 64-bit Windows.

Run the installer .exe file and keep default options. Make sure "Add Python to PATH" is enabled.

Open the command prompt and type `python --version` to verify Python installed correctly.

Mac OSX

Open a terminal window. Type `python3 --version` to check your pre-installed version.

If you're on Python 2.x, download the Python 3 installer pkg file from python.org.

Run the installer, keeping default options. This installs Python in addition to the system Python 2.

Test that Python 3 installed properly by typing `python3 --version` in terminal.

Linux (Debian/Ubuntu)

Open the terminal and check for Python with `python3 --version`. If you see "Python 3.x", you're all set!

If not installed, run `sudo apt update` then `sudo apt install python3` to install the latest Python 3 version.

Verify with `python3 --version`.

Python offers installers for other Linux distros and operating systems as well. Be sure to get Python 3 specifically, not legacy Python 2.

During installation, you can keep default options. The installer will add Python to your system PATH automatically so you can run it from the command line.

Once setup, you can confirm Python is installed and check the version with the `python --version` command. Make sure you get a Python 3.x version, not 2.x.

With Python installed, you're ready to start coding! But first, we need a proper code editor...

Installing a Code Editor

To write Python code, you need a quality code editor - not just Notepad or TextEdit. Good code editors provide features like:
- Code highlighting for easier reading
- Indentation and syntax help
- Debugging and error identification
- Addons and integrations for different languages

Popular free code editor options include:

Visual Studio Code: The most fully featured editor with abundant extensions

Atom: Created by GitHub, highly customizable and hackable

Sublime Text: Lightweight and speedy with time-saving features

Notepad++: Customized Notepad for Windows with extra functionality

We recommend Visual Studio Code as your editor. It has the richest feature set and most Python-specific capabilities. VS Code is free, open source, and runs on Windows, Mac, and Linux.

Here's how to install VS Code on different platforms:

Windows

Download the VS Code installer .exe from https://code.visualstudio.com/

Run the installer, keeping all defaults. This installs VS Code system-wide.

Open VS Code, select File > Open Folder, and create a project folder to store your code.

Mac

Go to https://code.visualstudio.com/ and download the VS Code .zip file for Mac.

Extract the zip anywhere you like. Drag Visual Studio Code to your Applications folder.

Launch VS Code. Select File > Open Folder to create a dev folder.

Linux

Go to: https://code.visualstudio.com/docs/setup/linux. Pick your distro's install steps.

The easiest method is usually through your distro's package manager. For example:

Debian/Ubuntu: `sudo apt install code`
Fedora: `sudo dnf install code`

Launch VS Code, select File > Open Folder, and make a project folder.

That covers the basic install! VS Code is highly customizable, and we'll discuss useful settings and extensions later on.

For now, you should have Python 3 and a code editor installed. You're ready to run your first script!

Your First Python Program

It is a tradition for beginning coders to write a simple "Hello World" program on their first day. This prints the text "Hello World!" to the screen and verifies your dev environment works.

Let's write our own Hello World in Python:

Launch VS Code and create a new file called `hello.py`

Now, type the following code:

```
print("Hello World!")
```

Save the file. Open your command prompt/terminal.

Navigate to the folder containing `hello.py`.

Run the command: `python hello.py`

You should see "Hello World!" output. Congrats, you just ran your first Python program!

Now let's break down what's happening here:

1. `hello.py` is our **script file** containing code
2. `print()` is a Python **function** that prints text
3. `"Hello World!"` is a **string** passed to print()
4. Running `python hello.py` **executes** the script

You've already seen some core programming concepts like functions, strings, and execution! We'll explore these ideas more starting next chapter.

As you continue learning Python, remember how far you've already come. It may feel daunting at first, but take it step-by-step. With the basics set up, you're ready to start coding for real.

In the next chapter, we'll dive into Python syntax basics - the lifeblood of your scripts. We'll look at variables, data types, operators, comments, and more. This will give you the building blocks to start writing Python that does useful things!

But for now, bask in the glory of getting set up and running your first program. Welcome to the world of coding!

Chapter 2 Summary

In this chapter, we:
- Learned what programming languages and code actually are
- Discussed why Python is an excellent first language to learn
- Installed Python 3 and the VS Code editor
- Wrote a simple "Hello World' script
- Ran our first Python program and printed output

With setup out of the way, we're ready to start digging into real Python syntax and concepts.

Coming up next in Chapter 2, we will learn about:
- Using variables to store data
- Python's core data types
- Arithmetic, comparison, and logical operators
- Indentation, comments, and code structure best practices

Let's start coding!

Chapter 3: Python Syntax and Structure

Introduction

Now that you have Python installed and have written your first script, we can dive into Python syntax basics.

In this chapter, we'll cover core elements like variables, data types, operators, indentation, and comments. These building blocks allow you to start writing Python that performs useful logic and tasks.

We will also create mini-programs to demonstrate these concepts in action. By the end, you'll have exposure to real Python code before applying it to larger projects. Let's get coding!

Variables and Data Types

A variable is like a box that stores data in your program's memory. You can store a value in a variable, then later retrieve or change it as needed. In Python, you don't need to declare a variable before assigning to it. Just choose a name and assign a value using:

```
# Assign string to variable
name = "Ada Lovelace"
```

```
# Reassign different value
name = "Marie Curie"
```

Variable names can contain letters, numbers, and underscores. They can't start with a number or contain spaces.

Naming Conventions

Variable names should be descriptive like student_count or temp_fahrenheit. Some naming conventions in Python include:

lower_case_with_underscores - Multiple words joined with underscores

CapitalizedWords - Class names use capital camel case

ALL_CAPS - Constants are capitalized

Avoid single letter names like X unless the purpose is obvious. Having meaningful names makes code more readable.

Data Types

Values have different data types in Python:

```python
Copy code
# Strings
name = "Carl Sagan"
```

```
# Integers
age = 45
```

```
# Floats (decimal numbers)
weight = 72.5
```

```
# Booleans
is_scientist = True
```

The main types you'll start with are:

- **Strings** - Text data like names. Use single or double quotes.
- **Integers** - Whole numbers like 3 or 25.
- **Floats** - Decimal numbers like 3.14 or 4.8.
- **Booleans** - True/false values for logic.

Python is **dynamically typed** so you don't declare types. Just assign values and Python sets the type automatically.

You can also check types using the `type()` function:

```
num = 15
print(type(num)) # Prints <class 'int'>
```

Later we'll cover more advanced types like lists, tuples, and dictionaries. But strings, numbers, and booleans make up the basics.

Now let's look at **type conversion** - converting between data types.

Type Conversion

You can convert between types like turning a string into an integer:

```
num_str = "456"
print(type(num_str)) # <class 'str'>
```

```
num_int = int(num_str)
print(type(num_int)) # <class 'int'>
```

Common conversions include:

`int()` - Convert to integer
`float()` - Convert to float
`str()` - Convert to string
`bool()` - Convert to boolean (True/False)

Here are some type conversion examples:

```
# String to int
num = int("35")
```

```
# Float to int loses decimal
int(3.14) # 3
```

```
# Boolean to int
int(True) # 1
int(False) # 0
```

```
# Int to string
str(42) # "42"
```

Now let's put variables and data types into practice...

Activity: Variables and Types

Create variables to store data for a famous scientist. Print their information:

```
name = "Marie Curie"
field = "Chemistry"
born = 1867
nobels = 2
```

```
print(name + " was a " + field + "
scientist born in " + str(born))
print("She won " + str(nobels) + " Nobel
Prizes")
```

This prints:

```
Marie Curie was a Chemistry scientist
born in 1867
She won 2 Nobel Prizes
```

We use + to concatenate strings. str() converts integers to strings for concatenation.

With variables and types, you can now store and print data in Python! Next let's look at manipulating data with operators.

Operators

Operators are symbols that perform actions on values and variables.
Python has operators for:

- Arithmetic (math)
- Comparison (logic)
- Assignment

Let's go through the common operators you'll use most.

Arithmetic Operators

Arithmetic operators apply standard math operations:

```
# Addition
1 + 1 # 2

# Subtraction
2 - 1 # 1

# Multiplication
2 * 3 # 6

# Division
6 / 2 # 3.0

# Floor division (discards decimal)
7 // 3 # 2

# Modulus (remainder)
7 % 3 # 1

# Exponent
2 ** 3 # 8 (2 to power of 3)
```

You can use arithmetic operators on any numeric data types like floats:

```
# Calculates pi
import math
radius = 3
circumference = 2 * math.pi * radius

print(circumference) # 18.8495559215
```

Next let's look at comparison operators which allow you to compare values.

Comparison Operators

Comparison operators evaluate to either True or False when comparing values:

```
# Equals
5 == 5 # True

# Not equals
5 != 6 # True

# Greater than
5 > 3 # True

# Less than
3 < 6 # True

# Greater than or equal
4 >= 4 # True

# Less than or equal
2 <= 4 # True
```

You can use comparisons to test conditions before running code:

```
age = 18
```

```
if age >= 18:
    print("You can vote!")
```

Other common comparisons include:

>, < - Greater/less than

>=, <= - Greater/less than or equal to

== - Equals

!= - Does not equal

is - Tests object identity

in - Checks for membership

We'll dive more into conditionals and comparisons later. But operators let you manipulate values right away.

Next let's quickly look at assignment operators.

Assignment Operators

The assignment operator = stores values in variables:

```
name = "Elon"
age = 50
```

Compound assignment operators like += combine an operation with assignment:

```
# Add and assign
points = 0
points += 100 # Same as points = points
+ 100

# Subtract and assign
lives = 3
lives -= 1 # Same as lives = lives - 1
```

This syntax is shorthand for updating variables. Other compound assignment operators include -=, *=, /=, etc.

With the main operators covered, you have the basic tools for manipulating data in your code. Let's see them in action...

Activity: Dog Years Calculator

Create a program that calculates a dog's age in "dog years" based on the popular myth that one human year equals 7 dog years.

Have the user input a dog's name and age. Then calculate and print the dog's age in human years and dog years:

```python
name = input("Enter your dog's name: ")
age = int(input("Enter your dog's age: "))

human_years = age
dog_years = age * 7

print(name + " is " + str(human_years) + " in human years")
print(name + " is " + str(dog_years) + " in dog years")
```

Example output:

```
Enter your dog's name: Rex
Enter your dog's age: 4

Rex is 4 in human years
Rex is 28 in dog years
```

This uses input() to get user data. We convert the input age to an integer since input is always a string. Then we multiply to calculate dog years.

With variables, data types, and operators down, we're starting to build real interactive programs! Now let's look at how to structure properly formatted Python code.

Indentation and Formatting

Unlike other languages that use brackets and semicolons, Python uses whitespace and indentation to structure code. This forces code to look clean and readable.

In Python, you must indent code blocks like functions, loops, and conditionals consistently based on their scope:

```python
# One level of indentation for this
function
def print_hello():

    # Two levels for this print() inside
the function
    print("Hello!")

# Back to one level indentation
print("Outside function")
```

Indentation Rules

Keep these Python indentation rules in mind:

- Indent using either spaces or tabs, but not both
- Most Python code indents 4 spaces
- Function and class definitions start with 0 indentation
- Code blocks start with 1 level of indentation (4 spaces)
- Nested blocks add another level (8 spaces, then 12 spaces, etc)
- Improper indentation causes an error
- In your code editor, you can press Tab to auto-indent. Set your editor to insert 4 spaces when pressing Tab for Python style.

The enforced indentation may seem strange at first. But consistent, clean indentation helps make code much more readable.

Other Style Guidelines

In addition to indentation, follow these style guidelines:

- Lines should be 79 characters max - Break up longer lines
- Use descriptive variable and function names

- Add comments to explain complex parts of code
- Import module statements at the top of files
- Use blank lines to separate sections and improve readability

These best practices will make your code neater and easier to understand. Now let's look at comments and docstrings - useful for documenting code.

Comments and Documentation

Comments allow you to add text descriptions and notes explaining your code. Python ignores comments when running your script.
You can add single line comments starting with #:

```python
# This initializes the variable x
x = 0
```

For longer multi-line comments, use triple quotes either ''' or """:

```python
'''This is a longer comment
   across multiple lines.
   Python ignores it when running.
'''
```

Comments are invaluable for explaining parts of complex code. Use them liberally so others (or your future self) can understand your scripts.

Docstrings

A special comment called a docstring describes how a function works:

```python
def calculate_area(radius):
    """Calculates the area of a circle
given radius."""
    area = 3.14 * radius ** 2
    return area
```

The docstring appears under the function definition as a multi-line comment. You can access it programatically with `function.__doc__`.

Docstrings provide excellent documentation for your functions. The Python style guide PEP 257 describes standards for writing good docstrings.

Now let's practice using comments and indentation...

Activity: Geometry Calculator

Write a program that calculates the area and perimeter for squares, rectangles, and circles based on user input:

```python
# Geometry calculator

# Functions to calculate area and
perimeter

def calculate_rectangle_area(length,
width):
    """Returns the area of a
rectangle."""
    return length * width

def
calculate_rectangle_perimeter(length,
width):
    """Returns the perimeter of a
rectangle."""
    return 2 * length + 2 * width

# Main user interaction

shape_type = input("Get area for what
shape (rectangle or circle): ")
```

```python
if shape_type == "rectangle":

    length = float(input("Enter length: "))
    width = float(input("Enter width: "))

    area = calculate_rectangle_area(length, width)
    perimeter = calculate_rectangle_perimeter(length, width)

elif shape_type == "circle":

    radius = float(input("Enter radius: "))

    # Import math module to use pi
    import math
    area = math.pi * radius ** 2
    perimeter = 2 * math.pi * radius

print("Area:", area)
print("Perimeter:", perimeter)
```

This program demonstrates:

- Defining reusable functions with docstrings
- Indenting code blocks like if statements
- Adding comments for explanation
- Importing modules

Proper code structure through indentation and comments ensures our code remains readable and maintainable.

Chapter 3 Summary

In this chapter, we covered core Python syntax fundamentals:
- Using variables to store values by data type
- Common operators like arithmetic, comparison, and assignment
- Correct indentation and spacing for code blocks
- Adding comments and docstrings to document code
- We also created mini-programs to apply these basics including a dog age calculator and geometry calculator.

With these building blocks, you can now start writing Python scripts that perform useful logic and tasks. In the next chapters, we'll expand on syntax and structure with:
- Control flow statements like if/else and loops
- Defining and using functions
- Working with data types like lists and dictionaries

For now, get familiar with playing around in Python and experimenting. Learn by doing!

Try small coding exercises like:
- A loan calculator that calculates monthly payments
- A weight converter that converts between pounds and kilograms
- A tip calculator that splits the bill for a dinner

Don't move forward until you feel comfortable with the basics covered so far. Variables, data types, and operators are the foundation of everything to come!

Chapter 4: Conditional Statements and Loops

Introduction

In this chapter, we'll explore control flow - making decisions and repeating code through conditionals and loops.

- Control flow gives your programs logic to respond intelligently based on different inputs and situations. We'll cover:
- If, else, and elif statements to execute code based on conditions
- While and for loops to repeat blocks of code
- Break, continue, and pass for additional loop control

By the end, you'll be able to write Python scripts that make decisions, iterate efficiently, and execute the right code at the right time. Let's dive in!

If, Else, and Elif Statements

Often you want code to execute only when certain conditions are met. An `if` statement runs code if its condition is True:

```
age = 18

if age >= 18:
  print("You can vote!")
```

This checks if `age` meets the condition `>= 18`. If so, it prints the message. The indented block under `if` runs only when the condition passes.

You can add an `else` block that executes if the condition is False:

```
age = 16

if age >= 18:
  print("You can vote!")
else:
  print("You cannot vote yet.")
```

Now different messages print depending on whether age passes the condition check.

For multiple conditions, `elif` (short for "else if") chains additional tests:

```
age = 12

if age >= 18:
  print("You can vote!")
elif age > 0:
  print("You're too young to vote.")
else:
  print("Invalid age.")
```

This tests each condition sequentially until one passes. It then executes that block and skips the remaining ones.

Some tips for conditionals:
- Indent the blocks under `if`, `elif`, and `else`
- Only use `elif` after an initial `if` statement

- You can include zero or more `elif` blocks
- The `else` block is optional

Now let's look at comparison operators we can use in conditionals.

Comparison Operators

Comparison operators compare two values and evaluate down to a single boolean - True or False:

```
5 > 3 # True
2 != 5 # True
7 >= 7 # True
```

We covered basic comparison operators like `>`, `==`, and `<=` in Chapter 2. Some additional useful operators include:

- `<` - Less than
- `<=` - Less than or equal to
  - `>` - Greater than
- `>=` - Greater than or equal to
- `==` - Equal to
- `!=` - Not equal
- `is` - Evaluates if both sides are the same object
- `in` - Checks if left value is in the right (like a list)

You can compare the types with typecasting functions:

```
age = 18
isinstance(age, int) # True

height = 5.5
isinstance(height, float) # True
```

This lets you check values are the expected type in conditionals.

Now let's see some examples combining conditionals and comparisons...

Check User Age

```
user_age = int(input("Enter your age: "))
```

```
if user_age >= 18:
  print("You are old enough to vote!")
elif user_age > 0:
  print("You cannot vote yet.")
else:
  print("Invalid age.")
```

This checks if a user-entered age meets voting requirements.

Validate Password

```
password = input("Enter a password: ")

if len(password) >= 8:
  print("Password accepted!")
else:
  print("Password too short - must be
8+ chars.")
```

Here we validate password length using the `len()` function.

Find the Larger Number

```
num1 = 800
num2 = 200

if num1 > num2:
  larger = num1
else:
  larger = num2

print("The larger number is:", larger)
```

A simple demo of comparing two values.

Conditionals like these let you control program flow based on logical checks. Next up - loops!

While Loops

A while loop runs as long as its condition remains True:

```
count = 0

while count < 5:
    print("Count:", count)
    count += 1
```

This prints Count: 0 up through Count: 4. The loop exits once count reaches 5.

The loop continually tests the condition each iteration. If you forget to update the variable being checked, the loop can run indefinitely in an infinite loop.

Here is the flow of execution for a while loop:

- Check condition
- If True, run body
- Go back to Step 1

Common patterns include:

- Initialize a counter variable
- Test it in the while condition
- Update the variable in the loop body
- You can break out early by setting the condition to False:

```
import random

random_num = random.randint(1, 10)  #
Random int 1-10
count = 0

while True:
```

```
    guess = int(input("Guess the number:
"))
    count += 1
    if guess == random_num:
        print("Correct!")
        break
```

We loop "forever" with `while True` then break when we guess correctly.

Now let's look at a few examples of while loops in action.

Count Up

Simple loop counting up:

```
x = 0

while x < 10:
    print(x)
    x += 1
```

Average Calculator

Calculate average of user inputs:

```
total = 0
count = 0

while True:
    user_num = input("Enter a number
('done' to finish): ")

    if user_num == 'done':
        break

    total += float(user_num)
    count += 1
```

```
average = total / count
print("Average:", average)
```

We break the loop by checking for a 'done' input.

Random Guessing Game

Guess a random number between 1-10:

```
import random

random_num = random.randint(1,10)
guess = None

while guess != random_num:
  guess = int(input("Guess the number:
"))

print("You guessed it!")
```

We loop until the user guesses correctly.

While loops let you repeat code indefinitely based on a condition. But often you'll want to iterate a fixed number of times using a for loop.

For Loops

A for loop iterates over a sequence of elements like a list or string:

```
fruits = ["apple", "banana", "cherry"]

for fruit in fruits:
  print(fruit)
```

This loops through and prints each fruit from the list.

The for loop variable iterates over each element, taking on its value. Any list, tuple, dictionary, or string can be used with for:

```python
# List
for num in [1, 2, 3]:
    print(num)

# Tuple
for letter in ('a', 'b', 'c'):
    print(letter)

# Dictionary
for k in {'a': 1, 'b': 2}:
    print(k)

# String
for char in "abc":
    print(char)
```

The `for` loop is flexible and commonly used in Python. You'll find yourself using it often!

Here are some `for` loop patterns and tips:

Use the `range()` function to iterate a fixed number of times:

```python
for i in range(5):
    print("Looping!", i)
```

You can start and stop at custom values:

```python
for i in range(3, 8):
    print(i) # Prints 3-7
```

Loop and modify items from a list:

```python
names = ["Bob", "Joe", "William"]

for name in names:
```

```
print(name.title())
```
Use `continue` and `break` for additional loop control
Now let's look at some examples that demonstrate more advanced
`for` loop techniques.

Sum a List

```
nums = [1, 2, 3, 4, 5]

total = 0
for num in nums:
    total += num

print(total) # 15
```
Uses the += assignment operator to sum values.

Find Primes

```
for num in range(2, 12):
    is_prime = True
    for factor in range(2, num):
        if num % factor == 0:
            is_prime = False

    if is_prime:
        print(num, "is prime!")
```
Nested loops check each number for factors - a common prime
number approach.

Caesar Cipher

```
text = "HELLO WORLD"

cipher_text = ""
for char in text:
    new_num = ord(char) + 3
```

```
    new_char = chr(new_num)
    cipher_text += new_char

print(cipher_text) # KHOOR ZRUOG
```

This simple encryption loops through and shifts characters by 3 letters. For loops provide a versatile way to iterate that you'll use all the time. But we can make them even more powerful with additional loop controls like break and continue.

Loop Control Statements

We've seen how break exits a loop immediately. Let's look at a few more statements for flexible loop control:

Break

Breaks out of the current loop:

```
for i in range(10):
    print(i)
    if i == 5:
        break # Exits loop
```

This prints 0-4 only. Useful for terminating loops early or in nested loops.

Continue

Skips the current iteration and goes to the next:

```
for i in range(10):

    # Go straight to next iteration
    if i % 2 == 0:
        continue

    print(i) # Prints odd numbers
```

Useful for skipping values in a loop without breaking entirely.

Pass

Does nothing and acts as a placeholder:

```
if x < 0:
    pass # TODO: handle negative values
```

You can use pass for stubbing out a block before adding the full logic.

Loop Else

Run a block if the loop ends normally without a break:

```
for i in range(5):
    if i == 3:
        break
else:
    print("Loop ended without breaking")
```

Don't use loop else often - typically break handles early exit.

These statements give you finer control over loop execution. Let's see an example combining a few controls...

Activity: Filtering a List

Use a loop and conditional statements to filter out negative numbers from a list and print the remaining numbers:

```
nums = [5, -3, 7, -2, 1, -8]

for num in nums:
    if num < 0:
        continue

    print(num)
```

This uses continue to skip negative values. We get:

```
5
7
1
```

The negative numbers got filtered out! Proper loop controls let you iterate flexibly.

We've now covered the core conditional and loop statements in Python. These tools allow you to:

- Make decisions and check conditions
- Repeat code efficiently
- Break down large problems into logical steps

You have the power to code intelligence into your programs! With practice, these constructs become second nature.

While loops and for loops serve similar purposes, but differ in their syntax and use cases:

While Loop	For Loop
Runs **while** condition is true	Iterates directly over elements
Condition tested on each iteration	Fixed number of iterations
Can run infinitely	Won't run infinitely
Use when number of iterations unknown	Use when number of iterations known

In upcoming chapters, we'll revisit conditionals and loops frequently. Mastering them opens up all kinds of programming possibilities!

Chapter 4 Summary

In this chapter, we covered:

- If, else, and elif statements for conditional code execution
- While loops to repeat code until a condition is met
- For loops to iterate over elements like lists and strings
- Break, continue, pass and other loop control statements

We saw how to use comparisons and logic to control program flow based on real conditions and constraints. With the ability to check conditions and repeat code, you can now build more advanced applications and simulate real program logic.

In the next chapter, we will learn how to define reusable functions to encapsulate code - further enhancing our Python skills!

Chapter 5: Functions and Modules

Introduction

In this chapter, we will explore functions and modules in Python.

Functions allow you to encapsulate code in reusable blocks with parameters and return values. Modules let you organize related functions, classes, and other code.

We will cover the following topics:
- Defining functions with def statements
- Arguments and parameters for passing data
- Return values from functions
- Local vs global variables scope
- Importing modules and standard libraries
- Creating custom modules to organize code

By the end, you'll be able to write clean, modular code by breaking programs down into logical reusable parts. Let's get started!

Defining Functions

A function definition outlines a block of reusable code with a name:

```
# Define function
def print_hello():
  print("Hello there!")

# Call function
print_hello() # Prints "Hello there!"
```

You define a function with `def name():` then indent the body. Call it by name with parentheses.

Functions encapsulate code you want to reuse. Let's look closer at the syntax:

```
# Parameters in parentheses
def function_name(param1, param2):

  # Function body
  statements

  # Optional return value
  return value
```

Parameters allow passing data into functions. Return sends data back out.

Functions also create a new **local scope** - variables inside are separate from the outside. Now let's look closer at parameters.

Function Parameters

Parameters allow passing arguments into a function:

```
# Parameters - names, age
def print_details(name, age):
```

```
   print(name + " is " + str(age) + "
years old.")

print_details("Monica", 25)
```

We define two parameters - name and age. When called, we pass the arguments "Monica" and 25 which get assigned to those parameters.

Parameters and arguments work similarly to regular variables:
- You can use any names for parameters
- Separate multiple parameters with commas
- Arguments passed must match the order of parameters
- Parameters get assigned the passed arguments
- By convention, parameters use snake_case like first_name while arguments can use any casing.

Let's see a few more examples of passing arguments to functions:

Print Full Name

```
def print_full_name(first, last):
    print(first.title() + " " +
last.title())

print_full_name("john", "doe") # John
Doe
print_full_name("mary", "smith") # Mary
Smith
```

Divide Two Numbers

```
def divide(dividend, divisor):
    if divisor != 0:
        print(dividend / divisor)
    else:
```

```
    print("Error: cannot divide by
zero.")

divide(10, 5) # 2.0
divide(15, 0) # Error message
```

Parameters give our functions flexibilty and reusability. Next let's look at return values.

Return Values

The return statement sends data back to the caller:

```
def multiply(num1, num2):
    return num1 * num2


product = multiply(2, 3)
print(product) # 6
```

- return exits the function immediately
- You can return any object - strings, lists, etc
- Return None by default if no return
- Calls can assign return value to variables
- Return keeps function internals hidden and returns only what's needed.

Let's look at various examples of returns:

Area of a Rectangle

```
def area(width, height):
    return width * height


rect_area = area(3, 4) # 12
```

Simple return of a calculation.

Validate Age

```
def check_driving_age(age):
```

```python
    if age >= 16:
        return True
    else:
        return False

can_drive = check_driving_age(18)
print(can_drive) # True
```

Returns booleans to indicate passing conditions.

Grade Calculator

```python
def calculate_grade(grade):

    if grade >= 90:
        return "A"
    elif grade >= 80:
        return "B"
    elif grade >= 70:
        return "C"
    else:
        return "F"

final_grade = calculate_grade(92)
print(final_grade) # A
```

Return strings representing different letter grades. Return allows functions to produce results that can be stored and used.

Variables Scope

Variables defined inside a function are in the local scope:

```python
def subtract(x, y):
```

```
    result = x - y
    return result

print(result) # Error, result isn't
defined
```

result only exists within the function after it's called.

Scope refers to where variables are available to be used:

Global scope - Available throughout the program

Local scope - Only available inside a function

You can access global variables from local scope, but not vice versa:

```
player_health = 100 # Global

def take_damage(damage):
    global player_health # Access global
    player_health -= damage

take_damage(25)
print(player_health) # Prints 75
```

Scope helps avoid unintended interactions between variables in different parts of a program.

Now that we've covered function basics like parameters, return, and scope, let uss see how to call functions themselves...

Calling Functions

You can call functions directly or store the results in variables:

```
# Direct call
print_hello()

# Call and assign
hello_str = print_hello()
```

print_hello() gets called either way.

Functions can also call other functions:

```python
def inches_to_feet(inches):
    return inches / 12

def feet_to_miles(feet):
    return feet / 5280

inches = 15000
feet = inches_to_feet(inches)
miles = feet_to_miles(feet)

print(miles)
```

The flow passes through two function calls for the conversion.

Calling the same function multiple times avoids duplicate logic:

```python
# Bad
print("Start")
print("Start")
print("Start")

# Good
def print_start():
    print("Start")

print_start()
print_start()
print_start()
```

Now that we've got functions down, it's time to look at modules!

Importing Modules

A module organizational code in a file. The Python standard library provides many useful modules:

```
import random

for i in range(5):
    value = random.randint(1, 6)
    print(value) # Prints random ints
```

`import module` imports the entire module

Call module functions with `module.func()`

Modules must be imported before using

You can import multiple modules on separate lines or together:

```
import math
import random
import statistics

print(math.pi)
print(random.randint(1,10))
```

Or import all into the current namespace with `from module import *`:

```
from math import *

print(pi) # No longer need math.pi
```

But this pollutes your namespace with more names.

Let's look at a few examples using common Python modules:

Random

```
import random

print(random.randint(1,10)) # Random int
```

```
print(random.choice([1, 2, 3])) #
Random element
print(random.shuffle([1, 2, 3])) #
Shuffles in place
```

Useful for games, simulations, AI, and more.

Math

```
import math

print(math.floor(2.7)) # 2
print(math.ceil(2.2)) # 3
print(math.sqrt(16)) # 4.0
```

Good for geometric, trigonometric, and numeric programming.

Statistics

```
from statistics import *

data = [1.5, 2, 2.5, 3, 3.5]
mean = mean(data)
median = median(data)

print(mean, median) # 2.5 2.5
```

Helpful modules for data analysis and scientific work.

Python's huge standard library has modules for practically any task. Now let's see how we can create our own.

Creating Modules

You can organize code into custom modules. Save modules as .py files:

```
# mathlib.py
```

```
def mean(values):
    return sum(values) / len(values)

def std_dev(values):
    avg = mean(values)
    return (sum([((x - avg) ** 2) for x
in values]) / len(values)) ** 0.5
```
You can then import your module:
```
import mathlib

vals = [1, 3, 4, 7]
print(mathlib.mean(vals))
print(mathlib.std_dev(vals))
```
This keeps related functions together in an importable file.

Some module tips:
- Use modules to organize related functions
- Modules can import other modules
- Put module files in the same directory as your scripts
- Name modules descriptively like mathlib.py
- Avoid circular imports between modules

Well organized modules and imports will keep your projects maintainable as they scale.

Chapter 5 Summary

In this chapter, we learned:
- How to define reusable functions with def statements
- Passing arguments with parameters and calling functions
- Returning values from functions
- Variable scope - global vs local
- Importing standard and custom modules
- Best practices for writing modular code

With functions and modules, we can:
- Encapsulate and reuse logic in functions
- Break programs down into logical parts
- Isolate variables and state to avoid conflicts
- Quickly access code in standard libraries
- Organize related functions together cleanly

Your ability to structure complex Python programs modularly will define your progression as a developer.

In upcoming chapters, we'll revisit functions often as we build larger programs and applications. Functions form the building blocks of Python projects.

Next we will start looking at more advanced data structures beyond strings, numbers and booleans. This will allow us to represent real world data more flexibly.

Get comfortable with writing functions and modules first before moving on. These skills open up the real power and organization of Python.

Happy coding!

Chapter 6: Working with Data

Introduction

In this chapter, we will go beyond basic data types and look at more advanced structures for organizing real world data in Python.

We will cover the following topics:
- Lists and tuples for ordered data
- Dictionaries and sets for unordered data
- Reading and writing files
- Methods for data manipulation
- Exception handling with try/except blocks

Learning these tools will allow you to load, represent, query, and write complex data in your programs.

Lists

A list represents an ordered sequence of data:

```
numbers = [1, 2, 3]
```

```
fruits = ["Apples", "Oranges",
"Bananas"]
```

Lists hold items that may be different types:

```
data = [1, "hello", 10.5, True]
```

Use [ ] brackets to create lists and commas , between items. Access elements by index starting at 0:

```
numbers = [5, 2, 3]
print(numbers[0]) # 5
print(numbers[1]) # 2
```

Lists support many built-in methods like append(), insert(), remove() etc:

```
fruits = ["apple", "orange"]
fruits.append("mango") # Append item to
end
fruits.insert(1, "banana") # Insert at
index
fruits.remove("orange") # Remove by
value
```

Lists are mutable - they can be modified after creating. This makes them useful for representing collections of data.

Now let's look at some common list operations and methods.

Access Items

```
animals = ["Lion", "Zebra", "Dolphin"]
first = animals[0]

last = animals[-1] # Get last item

animals[1] = "Giraffe" # Modify item
```

Lists allow flexible access and modification.

Append Items

```
sports = ["soccer", "football"]
sports.append("basketball") # Add new
item

print(sports) # ['soccer', 'football',
'basketball']
```

Append to add a new item to the end of a list.

Remove Items

```
colors = ["red", "green", "blue"]
colors.remove("green") # Remove by
value

print(colors) # ['red', 'blue']
```

Remove deletes an item by its value rather than index.

There are many more list methods to explore like sort(), copy(), pop(), etc. Lists form the backbone of many Python programs.

Tuples

A tuple is an immutable ordered sequence of items:

```
point = (2.5, 6.7)

# Can't modify tuples
point[0] = 5 # Error!
```

Tuples are like lists but can't be changed after creating. Construct with ( ) brackets instead of [ ] .

Tuples are useful when data shouldn't be modified, like coordinates or records:

```
student_record = ("John", "Physics",
3.5)
```

Trying to modify a tuple causes an error.
You can convert tuples to lists and vice versa:

```
tuple_1 = (1, 2, 3)
list_1 = list(tuple_1) # [1, 2, 3]

list_2 = [4, 5 ,6]
tuple_2 = tuple(list_2) # (4, 5, 6)
```

In summary, use tuples for fixed data and lists for mutable data. Next up - dictionaries!

Dictionaries

A dictionary maps keys to values like a real world dictionary maps words to definitions:

```
student = {
    "name": "Mark",
    "id": 15163,
    "gpa": 3.8
}

print(student["name"]) # Mark
print(student["id"]) # 15163
```

Dictionaries use key: value pairs inside { } braces. Values can be accessed by their key.

Keys must be unique and immutable like strings or numbers. Values can by anything:

```
student = {
    "name": "Sara",
    "classes": ["Math", "Physics"],
```

```
    "grades": {"Math": "A+", "Physics":
"A"}
}
```

Dictionaries have no inherent order since they use keys rather than indices.

Let's look at common dictionary methods:

Add or Modify

```
student = {
    "name": "Jean"
}

student["id"] = 15213 # Add new key-
value
student["name"] = "John" # Modify
existing
```

Assign to a new key to add it. Assign to existing key to modify.

Remove

```
student = {
    "name": "Alex",
    "id": 15321
}

student.pop("id") # Remove key "id"
```

Use pop(key) to remove a key-value pair.

Check Keys and Values

```
student = {
    "name": "Alice",
    "classes": ["Math", "CS"]
}
```

```python
print("name" in student) # True, key
exists
print("Math" in student["classes"]) #
True, value exists
```

Use `in` operator to check keys and values.

Dictionaries give us fast key-value lookup making them useful for many types of data.

Sets

A set is an unordered collection of unique items:

```python
numbers = {1, 2, 3}
fruits = {"apple", "banana", "orange"}
```

Sets use `{ }` braces but unlike dictionaries don't have key-value pairs. Items must be unique.

You can test for membership using `in`:

```python
numbers = {1, 2, 3}
print(2 in numbers) # True
```

Sets support set operations like unions, intersections, differences:

```python
math_students = {"Jane", "Mark",
"Tricia"}
cs_students = {"Akshay", "Tricia",
"Sarah"}

both = math_students & cs_students #
Intersection - {'Tricia'}
all_students = math_students |
cs_students # Union
```

Overall, here are common Python data structures and when to use them:

- **List** - Ordered collection, mutable
- **Tuple** - Ordered collection, immutable
- **Dictionary** - Unordered key-values, fast lookup
- **Set** - Unordered unique items

Different data types allow selectively picking the right datastructure for a particular purpose. Now that we can represent complex data, let's look at how to load and write it from files.

Reading and Writing Files

Python provides built-in open() for working with files on disk:

```
file = open("data.txt", "r") # Open for
reading
text = file.read() # Read entire
contents

lines = file.readlines() # Read line by
line
first = lines[0]

file.close() # Close when done
```

This loads a text file into memory. The "r" mode opens a file to read only.

Some other file modes include:
"r" - Read only
"w" - Write only (overwrite existing)
"a" - Append to existing
"r+" - Read and write

For writing, open with "w" or "a":

```
file = open("output.txt", "w")
file.write("Hello world!")
file.close()
```

This writes the text "Hello world!" to output.txt.

You can also use `with` statements to automatically close files:

```
with open("data.json", "r") as file:
    data = json.load(file) # Read json
format

print(data)
```

In summary:

- Use `open(file, mode)` to open files
- `open()` returns a file object
- Read with `.read()` or `.readlines()`
- Write with `.write()`
- Close when done with `.close()`
- `with` blocks auto close

Reading and writing files allows working with data from external sources.

Exception Handling

When executing programs, errors can occur unexpectedly. We should handle these gracefully using try/except blocks:

```
try:
    num = int(input("Enter a number: "))
except ValueError:
    print("That was not a valid number!")
```

If entering a non-number, the `ValueError` gets caught without crashing.

- `try` runs the code block being tested
- `except` catches any specified error types

- Multiple except blocks can be chained

This ensures the program doesn't crash every time an exception occurs.

Some common built-in exceptions:
- ImportError - Import fails
- ValueError - Type conversion failure
- ZeroDivisionError - Division by zero
- IOError - File not found
- TimeoutError - Operation exceeded time

You can catch specific exceptions or broad Exception parent class:

```
try:
    num = 5 / 0
except ZeroDivisionError:
    print("Can't divide by zero")
except Exception as e:
    print("Error!", e)
```

Here we catch the general case after specific ones. Make sure to handle exceptions appropriately in your programs.

Chapter 6 Summary

In this chapter, we learned about:
- Lists and tuples for storing ordered data
- Dictionaries and sets for unordered data
- Reading and writing files like CSVs and JSON
- Exceptions and handling errors gracefully
- Common data manipulation methods

You are now equipped to handle complex real-world data in Python, as you now know how to:
- Store data in powerful structures like lists and dicts
- Load datasets from external files
- Parse and transform data using Pythonic methods

- Handle errors smoothly when working with data
- Represent data in the optimal data type

With this foundation, you can build data-driven programs that handle CSV files, JSON APIs, database connections, user inputs, and more. Robust data handling will serve you well as you build larger Python applications.

In the next chapter, we will expand our Python skills into more intermediate topics and constructs. This will allow you to write more concise and "Pythonic" code.

Get comfortable with using files, dictionaries, exception handling, and more. These skills will be invaluable as you level up your Python abilities.

Chapter 7: Intermediate Python Concepts

Introduction

So far we've covered core Python basics like syntax, conditionals, functions, and data structures. In this chapter, we'll explore some more advanced features of Python to expand your skills.

We will now look at:
- List, dictionary, and set comprehensions
- Anonymous lambda functions
- Recursive functions
- First class functions with closures
- Object oriented programming basics
- Handling errors and exceptions

These topics will level up your abilities to write more advanced Python code. Let's get started!

List Comprehensions

List comprehensions provide a concise syntax for creating lists:

```python
nums = [x * 2 for x in range(10)]

print(nums)
# [0, 2, 4, 6, 8, 10, 12, 14, 16, 18]
```

This generates a list of doubles from 0-9. The equivalent for loop:

```python
nums = []
for x in range(10):
    nums.append(x * 2)
```

List comps have the basic syntax:

```python
[expr for val in collection]
```

Where:

`expr` is the expression to evaluate

`val` iterates over the `collection`

You can add `if` conditionals for filtering:

```python
evens = [x for x in range(20) if x % 2
== 0] # Even numbers

odds = [x for x in range(20) if x % 2
!= 0] # Odd numbers
```

List comps provide a more declarative way to create and filter lists compared to for loops.

Some other examples:

```python
# Square numbers
squares = [x**2 for x in range(10)]

# First letter
names = ["Elise", "Bob", "Alice"]
first_initials = [name[0] for name in
names]
```

```
# Filter numbers
nums = [1, -2, 3, -4, 5]
positives = [num for num in nums if num
> 0]
```

When you need to build lists, consider using list comprehensions for cleaner code.

Dictionary and Set Comprehensions

Dictionaries and sets also support comprehension syntax:

```
# Dictionary comprehension
values = {x: x**2 for x in range(5)}
print(values) # {0: 0, 1: 1, 2: 4, 3:
9, 4: 16}

# Set comprehension
values = {x**2 for x in range(10)}
print(values) # {0, 1, 4, 9, 16, 25,
36, 49, 64, 81}
```

These create dicts and sets in a similar way to list comps.
Comprehensions provide a more Pythonic alternative to verbose for loops for all data collections.

Anonymous Lambda Functions

Python supports small anonymous functions called lambda functions:

```
double = lambda x: x * 2
print(double(7)) # 14
```

lambda declares an anonymous inline function

These functions accepts any number of args but only have one expression, and are handy for short logic you need to pass around.

Lambdas benefit from avoiding repetitive small function definitions. You'll often pass lambdas to other functions that expect callable arguments. Like with `map()`:

```
nums = [2, 4, 6]

doubled = map(lambda x: x*2, nums)
print(list(doubled)) # [4, 8, 12]
```

`map` applies the lambda to each list item. Lambdas allow coding simple one-liners instead of full functions.

Some key facts about lambda functions:
- Also called anonymous functions because they have no name
- Useful for short bits of logic you need to pass around
- More constrained than regular `def` functions
- Avoid complex lambdas - use `def` instead for clarity

Let's look at a couple more examples of lambdas:

Filter List

```
vals = [1, 2, 3, 4, 5, 6]

evens = list(filter(lambda x: x % 2 ==
0, vals))

print(evens) # [2, 4, 6]
```

Filters to even values using filter + lambda.

Sort List

```
products = [("Phone", 150), ("PC",
1200), ("Tablet", 400)]
```

```python
sorted_products = sorted(products,
key=lambda x: x[1])

print(sorted_products)
# [('Phone', 150), ('Tablet', 400),
('PC', 1200)]
```

Sorts products by price from low to high.

Lambdas are one of those Pythonic features that take your code to the next level. Now let's look at recursion - functions that call themselves.

Recursive Functions

Recursion is when a function calls itself to repeat an operation:

```python
def factorial(n):
    if n == 1:
        return 1
    else:
        return n * factorial(n-1)

print(factorial(5)) # 120
```

This calculates a factorial recursively. The flow:

- Base case - the stopping condition `return 1`
- Recursive call - `factorial(n-1)` calls itself

Recursion works well for:

- Tasks with repetitive subproblems
- Tree structures
- Mathematical sequences
- Sorting algorithms

The recursive Fibonacci sequence:

```python
def fib(n):
```

```
if n <= 2:
    return 1
else:
    return fib(n-1) + fib(n-2)
```

Be careful with recursion depth since it adds a new stack frame per call.

Next let's look at treating functions as first class objects.

First Class Functions

In Python, functions are considered "first class" - they can be used like any other object:

- Stored in variables and data structures
- Accepted as arguments to other functions
- Returned as values from other functions

For example, we can store functions:

```
def add(a, b):
    return a + b

sum = add # Assign function

print(sum(5, 2)) # 7
```

And pass as arguments:

```
def execute(func, a, b):
    return func(a, b)

def subtract(a, b):
    return a - b

print(execute(subtract, 8, 4)) # 4
```

Inner functions can also access variables in parent scopes. These are called closures:

```
def outer():

    x = 5

    def inner():
        print(x)

    inner()

outer() # Prints 5
```

`inner()` accesses the parent `x` without taking it as an argument.

Overall, functions in Python offer a lot of power and flexibility through features like treating them as objects.

Classes and Objects

Python supports object oriented programming (OOP) through class definitions and constructor instantiation:

```
class Person:

    def __init__(self, name, age):
        self.name = name
        self.age = age

    def greeting(self):
        print(f"Hello, my name is
{self.name}")

john = Person("John", 36)
john.greeting()
```

`class` defines a class with data and methods
`__init__` constructor method initializes instances
`self` references the created instance

Objects encapsulate data and behavior
Classes model real world entities like users, products, etc. You can create multiple instances with unique data.

Instances get their own copies of data attributes and methods. Let's enhance the Person with more fields, properties, and methods:

```python
class Person:

    def __init__(self, name, age):
        self.name = name
        self.age = age

    @property
    def name(self):
        return self._name

    @name.setter
    def name(self, name):
        if len(name) < 2:
            raise ValueError("Name is too short")
        self._name = name

    def greeting(self):
        print(f"Hello, my name is {self.name}")
```

```
    def age_next_year(self):
        return self.age + 1

john = Person("John", 36)
print(john.age_next_year()) # 37
john.name = "J" # Raises ValueError
```

We've added:

A name property with getter and setter

age_next_year() method that uses self

Custom validation in @name.setter

This demonstrates classes encapsulating logic related to the Person entity.

Now you can model real world domains! We've just scratched the surface of OOP - you'll continue discovering powerful techniques and design patterns with experience.

Next let's revisit exceptions and handling errors robustly.

Handling Errors

It's important to handle errors gracefully in larger programs using try/except blocks:

```
try:
    num = int(input("Enter a number: "))
    print(100 / num)
except ValueError:
    print("You did not enter a valid
number")
except ZeroDivisionError:
    print("Cannot divide by zero")
```

This handles two different errors specific to the use case.

You want to catch and recover from errors so the overall program flow isn't interrupted. Key points to note:
- Wrap risky code in `try` blocks
- Catch expected errors with `except` and handle
- Specify multiple `except` blocks from specific to general
- Use built-in error classes like ValueError, TypeError
- Don't silence errors or hide with bare `except` clauses

Handling errors robustly will ensure your programs don't go down for expected issues.

Chapter 7 Summary

In this chapter, we learned:
- Comprehensions for concise data list, dict, and set creation
- Anonymous lambda functions for throwaway logic
- Recursive functions that call themselves
- Treating functions as objects with closures and passing
- Object oriented programming basics with classes
- Robust error handling practices using try/except blocks

These more advanced concepts will allow you to:
- Write more Pythonic code following language best practices
- Build complex systems using object oriented principles
- Handle errors smoothly so programs can recover
- Take advantage of Python features like first-class functions
- Create concise but readable code with comprehensions

With these intermediate skills, you can build larger systems and write more idiomatic Python code. Master these techniques through practice and reviewing examples.

Soon you will be ready to start building real world Python applications and tools. But first, let's solidify your understanding of topics covered up to this point.

For future success, focus on:

- Writing robust scalable functions
- Creating classes to model complex systems
- Handling all errors gracefully
- Breaking problems down systematically
- Picking the right data structures and algorithms

The topics covered will serve as an invaluable foundation as you advance to completing real Python projects.

Chapter 8: Building Python Projects

Introduction

We've now covered all the main Python concepts from basic syntax and data types to classes and exceptions. In this chapter, we'll integrate everything you've learned to build real world Python programs.

Project-based learning will solidify your Python skills and let you create an impressive coding portfolio. We'll build:
- A command line calculator app
- A text-based adventure game
- A web scraper to extract data
- Data visualizations with Matplotlib
- A CRUD application with file database

These projects will show you how all the pieces fit together into complex applications. Let's get started!

Project #1: Calculator

Let's start with a simple command line calculator app that takes user input and evaluates math expressions.

Step 1: Handle Input

We'll use `input()` to get the calculation string and `eval()` to evaluate it:

```python
expression = input("Enter an expression: ")
result = eval(expression)
print(result)
```

`eval()` interprets the string as actual Python code, evaluating the expression.

Step 2: Loop for Multiple Expressions

Allow entering multiple expressions in a loop:

```python
while True:
    expression = input("Enter an expression: ")
    result = eval(expression)
    print(result)
```

We loop forever until the user manually exits.

Step 3: Handle Errors

Add try/except blocks to handle any errors:

```python
while True:
    expression = input("Enter an expression: ")

    try:
        result = eval(expression)
        print(result)
    except NameError:
        print("Invalid expression")
    except:
```

```
    print("Error evaluating
expression")
```

We catch a general error in calculating the result.

And that's it! Our calculator accepts expressions like "5 + 5" or "2 ** 3", doing the math and printing the result.

To expand this further:
- Allow multiple expressions separated by comma
- Limit expressions from running too long with recursion
- Add unit conversions like Celsius to Fahrenheit
- Import math module for extra functions like sin()

An interactive command line calculator makes for a simple but useful coding project. Next up, a text adventure game!

Project #2: Text Adventure Game

For this project we'll build an interactive text-based adventure game. The program presents scenarios and choices, responds based on user input, and displays engrossing narrative text. We'll build it modularly with classes, functions, conditionals, and data structures.

Step 1: Game Intro and Setup

Print an intro message and get the player's name:

```
print("Welcome to the adventure!")
name = input("Enter your name: ")
print(f"Hello {name}! Let's start your
adventure...")
```

Prompt for choices using input() based on the current point in the story.

Step 2: Story and Choices

Define functions for each story snippet. Pass the player name:

```
def start_adventure(name):
    print(f"{name}, you are on a long
journey to the ancient temple...")
```

```python
    choice = input("Do you go left or
right? ").lower()
    if choice == 'left':
        go_left(name)
    elif choice == 'right':
        go_right(name)
    else:
        invalid_choice(name)

def go_left(name):
    print(f"{name}, you come across a
forest.")
    # Continue story...
```

We prompt the user and move the story forward based on their input.

Step 3: Inventory System

Track collected items in a list:

```python
inventory = []

# User collects an item
inventory.append("sword")
print(f"Inventory: {inventory}")
```

Check if items are in inventory for certain actions:

```python
if "sword" in inventory:
    print("You fight the monster with
your sword!")
```

Step 4: Game Classes

Use OOP with classes for players, items, and enemies:

```python
class Player:

    def __init__(self, name):
```

```
    self.name = name
    self.inventory = []

  def add_item(self, item):
    self.inventory.append(item)

player = Player(name)
player.add_item("sword")
```

This helps encapsulate related data and behavior.

The full game combines strings, variables, lists, conditionals, loops, functions, and classes into an interactive program. Text-based games force you to handle complex logic and state.

To expand the game:
- Add statistics like health and currency
- Save/load functionality using files
- More items, enemies, places, and story branches
- Improve text formatting for readability

This type of project lets you flex your coding creativity! Next up, extracting data from the web.

Project #3: Web Scraper

For this project, we'll build a simple web scraper to extract data from a website. We'll use the requests and Beautiful Soup libraries.

The goal is to extract job titles and links from the Python jobs listing on RealPython.com.

Step 1: Request Page HTML
Use requests to download the page:

```
import requests
```

```
base_url =
"https://realpython.com/jobs/results/"
r = requests.get(base_url)
page_html = r.text
```

This stores the HTML source in a string.

Step 2: Parse HTML

Use Beautiful Soup to parse and process the HTML:

```
from bs4 import BeautifulSoup

page_soup = BeautifulSoup(page_html,
"html.parser")
page_soup.prettify() # Formatted HTML
```

We can search, navigate, and extract data from the parsed HTML.

Step 3: Extract Job Data

Find job elements and extract parts:

```
jobs = page_soup.find_all("h2",
class_="job-listing")

for job in jobs:
    title = job.find("a").text.strip()
    link = job.find("a")['href']

    print(title, link)
```

This locates the job list elements, gets the title and link, and prints the data.

We could also save the data to a CSV or database. Additionally, the program can scrape multiple pages by appending page numbers to the URL.

To expand this:
* Extract additional metadata like company and location

- Save data to a CSV, JSON, or database file
- Add exception handling for robustness
- Scrape additional info from each job page

Web scraping demonstrates real world data extraction and processing in Python. Let's switch gears now to data visualization.

Project #4: Data Visualization

For this project, we'll use Matplotlib to build visualizations from data. We'll cover bar charts, histograms, scatter plots, and more.

Step 1: Imports and Data

```
from matplotlib import pyplot as plt
import random

values = [random.randint(1, 100) for i
in range(100)]
```

This generates some random data to plot.

Step 2: Bar Chart

Plot data in a simple bar chart:

```
plt.bar(range(len(values)), values)
plt.title("Bar Chart")
plt.xlabel("Index")
plt.ylabel("Value")
plt.show()
```

Customize the chart labels, legend, axis, etc.

Step 3: Histograms

Plot a histogram showing value distributions:

```
plt.hist(values)
plt.title("Histogram")
plt.xlabel("Value")
plt.ylabel("Frequency")
```

```
plt.show()
```
Histograms visualize data spreads and patterns.

Step 4: Scatter Plots

Plot x,y coordinate data in a scatter plot:

```
x_values = range(100)
y_values = [x ** 2 for x in x_values]

plt.scatter(x_values, y_values)
plt.title("Scatter Plot")
plt.xlabel('X Coordinate')
plt.ylabel('Y Coordinate')
plt.show()
```
Scatter plots reveal relationships between two data sets.

Matplotlib supports many plot types like pie charts, area plots, 3D graphs, and Geographic maps. The data can come from files, databases, web APIs, sensors, or user inputs.

To expand this:
- Build an interactive dashboard with multiple visualizations
- Connect charts to live data sources that update
- Allow users to customize charts through UI options
- Add animations and transitions

Data visualization projects let you present information visually and extract insights. Finally let's look at a database-backed app.

Project #5: CRUD Web App

For our final project, we'll build a web application that performs CRUD (create, read, update, delete) functions on data.

We'll use the Flask framework and store data locally in a JSON file.

Step 1: Database Setup

Initialize an empty JSON file for our database:

```
database.json
```

```
{"users": []}
```

The users array will store user data as dicts.

Step 2: Flask Routes

Set up Flask app and routes for each CRUD operation:

```python
from flask import Flask
import json

app = Flask(__name__)

@app.route("/users")
def get_users():
    # Open and return database
    pass

@app.route("/users", methods=['POST'])
def create_user():
    # Add new user to database
    pass

@app.route("/users/<int:user_id>",
methods=['PUT'])
def update_user(user_id):
    # Update user in database
    pass

@app.route("/users/<int:user_id>",
methods=['DELETE'])
```

```
def delete_user(user_id):
    # Delete user from database
    pass
```

These tie URLs to Python functions to execute operations.

Step 3: Implement Functionality

Flesh out the functions to manipulate the JSON file:

```
import json

# Open database.json
with open("database.json") as file:
    data = json.load(file)

# Get all users
def get_users():
    return {"users": data["users"]}

# Add new user
def create_user(user):
    data["users"].append(user)
    save_db()

# Save updated data
def save_db():
    with open("database.json", "w") as f:
        json.dump(data, f)
```

We load data, manipulate it, and save changes back to the file database.

The full CRUD app ties together Flask APIs, a JSON file datastore, and Python data manipulation logic. The same principles apply for app backends connected to real databases.

To expand this:
- Add a frontend UI with forms and data tables
- Connect to a Mongo, MySQL, or PostgreSQL database
- Add authentication and authorization
- Deploy the web app so it's publicly accessible

CRUD apps form the backbone of many real world web and mobile applications.

Chapter 8 Summary

In this chapter, we built real Python programs from scratch:
- An interactive command line calculator
- A text adventure game with OOP
- A web scraper to extract jobs data
- Data visualizations with Matplotlib
- A CRUD app with Flask APIs and file datastore

These projects showed you how to:
- Combine everything you've learned into complex programs
- Break problems down into logical components
- Use Python standard libaries for real world tasks
- Build apps that integrate data, APIs, frontends, and UIs
- Apply Python to real world use cases beyond just coding exercises

With these skills, you can now build a diverse portfolio of projects to grow your Python skills, demonstrate them, and solve real problems.

The possibilities are endless! Some ideas for projects:
- Virtual assistant chatbot with NLP
- Social media bot that interacts with Twitter
- Web application with Flask and front end
- Automated scripts for tasks and workflows
- Machine learning model training app
- Mini games with PyGame

- Productivity tools and apps

Learning by creating projects gives you an engaging way to confirm your Python proficiency. It also lets you express creativity and build useful tools.

Chapter 9: Moving Forward

Introduction

Throughout this book, you've learned beginner to intermediate level Python skills. In this final chapter, we'll discuss next steps to continue advancing as a Python programmer.

You're now equipped with:

- Knowledge of Python basics like data structures, functions, classes
- Ability to build real world programs from scratch
- Problem solving and critical thinking strategies
- Experience creating your own modules and packages
- Familiarity with portions of Python's extensive standard library

Where you go from here depends on your own goals and interests. Let's explore some recommendations for further developing your Python abilities.

Expanding Your Python Skills

Python is a huge language with far more to uncover than we could cover in this introductory text. Here are some recommendations for continuing to expand your Python knowledge:

Learn More Libraries and Frameworks

While we covered critical core libraries like requests and BeautifulSoup, there are dozens more specialized libraries to explore. For example:

- **NumPy** - Foundational package for scientific computing and data analysis using arrays and matrices. Works well with Pandas.
- **Pandas** - Data analysis and manipulation tool built on NumPy. Excellent for working with tabular data.
- **Django** - Leading web framework for building browser-based web applications.
- **Flask** - Microframework for building Python web apps and APIs.
- **Tensorflow** - End-to-end open source platform for machine learning from Google.

Each of these libraries has its own ecosystem and set of capabilities. Learning them expands what you can build with Python.

Dig Into More Advanced Python Features

Python has many other built-in features we didn't cover including:
- Decorators for modifying functions
- More advanced OOP like inheritance
- Generators and iterators
- Metaprogramming for modifying code
- Multi-threading and async programming
- Custom context managers

Mastering these unlocks new techniques for writing Pythonic code.

Practice and Learn by Doing

There's no better way to reinforce skills than hands-on practice and building projects. Some ideas:

- Expand your portfolio with unique, complex projects
- Enter hackathons to build something new under a time constraint
- Recreate popular apps and tools using Python
- Find open source Python projects to contribute to
- Follow tutorials to learn specific skills
- Expand abilities through online Python challenges

Choose projects aligned with your interests to stay engaged and having fun!

Read Others' Python Code

Reading code is one of the best ways to learn. Exposure to well-written, properly styled Python will improve your own coding habits.

Ways to read Python code:

- Study open source projects on GitHub
- Step through code samples in documentation
- Debug projects by reading through the codebase
- Run Python programs line-by-line in an interpreter
- Participate in code reviews and examine teammates' code

The more quality Python code you read, the more Pythonic patterns you'll internalize.

Pursuing these avenues will continue advancing you towards Python mastery. Next let's look at getting involved in the Python community.

Joining the Python Community

One of Python's greatest strengths is its large, welcoming community. Here are some ways to get involved:

Attend Local Meetup Groups

Most major cities have Python meetup groups that host in-person and virtual events. These provide opportunities to:
Meet fellow Python programmers
Attend tech talks and workshops
Showcase projects and get feedback
Hear about local job opportunities
Socialize and code with other Pythonistas!
Meeting local users keeps you engaged and learning.

Join Python Forums and Chat Rooms

Forums like Reddit's r/Python have endless discussions and queries. Chat rooms like Python on Gitter let you ask questions and interact in real time.

Other places to get Python community support:
- Stack Overflow python tag
- PyDiscourse forum
- Python subreddit
- Python Discord servers

Quickly get help debugging issues or guidance on best practices.

Attend or Volunteer at Python Conferences

Major conferences like PyCon US, PyCon Canada, and EuroPython connect thousands of developers. These feature keynote talks, breakout sessions, networking events, and more.

Can't attend in-person? Look for virtual conferences and live-streamed talks.

You can also volunteer at conferences which is a great way to support and connect with the community. Help organize, introduce speakers, manage A/V, or assist at info booths.

Follow Python News and Updates

Keep up with the latest Python happenings through:
- r/Python subreddit
- Python Weekly and PyCoder's Weekly newsletters
- RealPython and Dice Insights blogs
- TalkPython and Podcast.**init** podcasts
- Twitter #python hashtag and experts like @raymondh, @gvanrossum, @pypi etc

This helps you stay on top of new library releases, Conference dates, Python trends, and more.

Immersing yourself in the Python community accelerates learning while making programming enjoyable. Next let's look at contributing to open source.

Contributing to Open Source

Contributing to open source Python projects lets you give back while honing skills. You'll improve at:
- Reading and understanding large codebases
- Debugging and troubleshooting issues
- Following style guides and best practices
- Communicating through GitHub issues and pull requests
- Reviewing other's code effectively
- Documenting projects
- Building features and fixes for production use

Even small contributions help and are highly valued by maintainers. Here are starter ways to contribute:

Report Issues and Bug Fixes

If you find a bug while using an open source project - report it! The best bug reports provide:

- Detailed steps to reproduce the issue
- Examples of the problem
- The environment, OS, Python version used
- Screenshots, logs, or snippets exhibiting the bug

For extra credit, you can submit a pull request resolving the bug. Fixing typos and documentation errors also helps.

Suggest Enhancements and Improvements

Is a library missing a common feature? Does the docs need clarification? Propose your ideas for improvements through issues and discussions. Some easy ways you can do this:

- Outline your suggested enhancement with reasoning and examples
- Offer to implement it in a pull request
- Ask if maintainers are open to the idea before diving in
- Even if declined, you help expand maintainers' perspectives.

Create Examples and Improve Documentation

Most projects need more good examples and documentation. You can quickly improve these:

- Add code snippets demonstrating library usage
- Expand class and function docstrings with details
- Proofread docs and fix typos
- Clarify confusing documentation
- Create diagrams, graphics, or videos

This makes the project more accessible to other learners.

Donate to Project Funding

Many projects accept financial donations through Open Collective, GitHub Sponsors or elsewhere. Even small donations help cover domain costs, hosting, etc.

Larger projects may fundraise for contractors, events and meetups. Chip in what you can to democratize development.

The beauty of open source is anyone can contribute meaningfully. Don't be intimidated to start small! Next we'll explore Python career paths.

Python Careers

Once you have intermediate to advanced Python skills, exciting career opportunities open up. Common Python roles include:

Web Developer

Build scalable web apps and APIs using frameworks like Django, Flask, and FastAPI. Integrate front ends, databases, servers, testing, and deployment.

Data Scientist / Data Engineer

Use Python for statistical analysis, machine learning, predictive analytics, and managing big data platforms.

DevOps Engineer

Automate operational processes like infrastructure provisioning, configuration management, CI/CD pipelines, and monitoring using Python scripting and tools.

Security Engineer

Perform penetration testing, vulnerability assessments, and forensic analysis of systems and networks using Python. Automate security processes.

Product/Project Manager

Manage technology projects end-to-end. Technical knowledge helps oversee technical specs and timelines.

Researcher / Academic

Python's versatility across domains makes it ubiquitous in academic research and development.

With some experience, you can begin applying for Python roles or internships. Here are tips for advancing your career:
- Beef up your portfolio with diverse Python projects

- Contribute to open source projects
- Attend hackathons and coding events
- Expand skills through MOOCs like from Udemy or Coursera
- Consider a computer science or related degree
- Get certified through tests like PCEP Python from the PCEP Program
- Attend local meetups and network with professionals
- Apply to Python jobs and internships

The more skills and experience you gain, the more qualified you become. With passion and some hustle, you can land a Python job you love!

Chapter 9 Summary

In this final chapter, we discussed next steps and resources for:
- Continuing to improve your Python skills through practice and learning advanced topics
- Getting involved in the Python community through conferences, meetups, and open source
- Potential Python career paths in web development, data science, DevOps, and more

With the foundation you've built, you're well on your way to Python mastery! Keep growing through:
- Creating and contributing - nothing teaches coding better
- Reading others' code and docs to expose yourself to great Python
- Joining Python forums and events to engage with the community
- Experimenting with new libraries and techniques outside your comfort zone
- Building real-world products, tools, models, and apps that help people

Thank you for following along this Python journey with me! It's been a pleasure guiding you from beginner to intermediate.

I am excited to see where you take your newfound skills - the possibilities are endless! Remember to enjoy the coding journey - learn, grow, build, and repeat.

Now go share your Python creations with the world!

Conclusion

Here is a summary of the key topics we covered in this Python programming book:

Python Basics

Variables, data types, operators
Strings, numbers, booleans
Lists, tuples, dicts, sets
Control flow with conditionals and loops
Functions to encapsulate reusable logic
Exceptions for handling errors

Intermediate Concepts

Comprehensions for elegant data manipulation
Anonymous lambda functions
Recursive functions calling themselves
First class functions treated as objects
Intro to object oriented programming
Robust error handling with try/except blocks

Projects

Calculator command line app
Text adventure game with classes
Web scraper with requests and Beautiful Soup
Data visualizations with Matplotlib
CRUD application with Flask and file database

Along the way you learned:

- How to think programmatically and break problems down
- Pythonic techniques like list comprehensions
- Building modules and well-structured code
- Basics of using classes for modeling data
- Powerful methods for handling complex data
- Fundamentals of APIs, GUIs, and web dev
- How to expand your skills through projects

The intermediate skills you've gained will serve as a strong foundation for building real world apps, tools, AI systems and more. You're now set up for a bright future in Python!

Some recommendations as you continue your coding journey:
- Practice by recreating projects from scratch
- Expand skills through Python challenges and exercises
- Learn more advanced Python features and libraries
- Get comfortable reading others' Python code
- Continue building portfolio projects
- Participate in open source projects on GitHub
- Consider a CS degree or Python certification

With commitment and practice, you can take your Python abilities to the next level. Python is a skill that will pay dividends for decades to come as technology continues to evolve.

A Final Word

I truly appreciate your participation in this unique journey. your teenage years be filled with the joy of wonder, discovery, and limitless potential, as you deploy your newfound knowledge of Python.

If you liked this book, please help me spread the word by:

- Leaving a 5-star review on Amazon
- Telling your siblings, classmates, friends and relatives about this book

- Recommending this book to your teacher, coach or educator, and
- Sharing your thoughts on social media

Last but not least, do check out our other titles and stay tuned for new and exciting releases from Lexicon Labs. Some of them are highlighted in the pages that follow.

I wish you lots of good luck and lots of new adventures!

Dr. Leo Lexicon

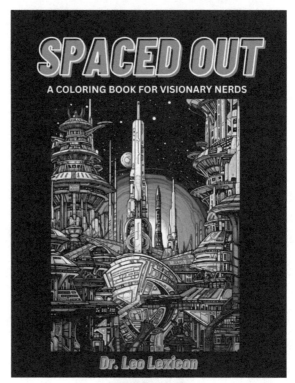

Check out our fun, auto-themed coloring books

Hours of coloring fun for all ages!

 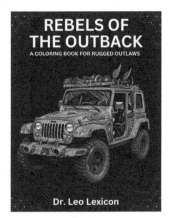

- Each book has over 40+ carefully curated HQ images
- Pefect companion for a road trip or vacation
- Try one today, you won't be disappointed
- Check out our other titles, we have all ages covered
- From the team at Lexicon Labs, bringing joy one page at a time!
- Follow Dr. Leo Lexicon on Twitter

 @LeoLexicon

LEXICON LABS

Discover More Bestselling Titles from Lexicon Labs!

SCAN ME

Made in United States
Troutdale, OR
10/11/2023